# Contents

# What is food?

Food is everything that we eat.

We eat lots of different foods.

# Living things and food

People, other animals, and plants
are living things.

All living things need food.

# Plant food

Plants make their own food.

Plants use water, air, and sunlight to make food.

# Animal food

Some animals eat plants.

Cows eat grass.

Some animals eat other animals.

Owls eat mice.

Some animals eat other animals
and plants.

Some people eat meat
and vegetables.

# Why do living things need food?

People and other animals need food to stay alive.

Plants need food to stay alive, too.

Food gives living things energy.

Living things need energy to move.

Living things need energy to keep warm.

Living things need energy to grow.

# Food quiz

Which of these things does not need food?

Answer on page 24

# Picture glossary

**energy**  the power to do things. Living things need energy to move, keep warm, and grow.

**living thing**  something that is alive, such as an animal or a plant

# Index

**Answer to question on page 22**
The cat and the girl need food.
The wall does not need food.

**Notes for parents and teachers**

**Before reading**

Ask the children to tell you their favourite food. Write their suggestions on paper to make a poster. Ask the children why they think it is important to eat food. Add their ideas to the poster. Explain why all living things need food. If the children are ready, discuss food chains. Plants make their own food and so are at the start of all the food chains.

**After reading**

- Cut out pictures of animals, including people, and paste them onto pieces of card. Do the same with pictures showing food those animals would eat. Ask each child to choose an animal card. Lay out the food cards face up and tell the children to take turns to select a food their animal would eat. If they cannot see a suitable card, ask them to suggest a food and write this onto a new piece of card. Discuss their choices.
- Divide the cards above into "food" and "animal" piles. Give one child the animal cards and another the food cards. The children should take turns to turn over a card from their pile. They should call out "Snap!" if the animal would eat the food shown. The first child to call out correctly takes the matching pair. The winner is the child with the most pairs after all the cards have been turned over.